Flirt

D0830659

MARY BURRITT CHRISTIANSEN POETRY SERIES

Hilda Raz, Series Editor

Mary Burritt
Christiansen
Poetry Series

Also available in the University of New Mexico Press
Mary Burritt Christiansen Poetry Series:

Flirt

Noah Blaustein

[signature]

9-9-13

UNIVERSITY OF NEW MEXICO PRESS

ALBUQUERQUE

© 2013 by the University of New Mexico Press
All rights reserved. Published 2013
Printed in the United States of America

18 17 16 15 14 13   1 2 3 4 5 6

Library of Congress Cataloging-in-Publication Data

Blaustein, Noah, 1969–
 [Poems. Selections]
 Flirt / Noah Blaustein.
    pages cm. — (Mary Burritt Christiansen Poetry Series)
 Poems.
 ISBN 978-0-8263-5383-2 (pbk. : alk. paper) — ISBN 978-0-8263-5384-9 (electronic)
 I. Title.
 PS3602.L399F55 2013
 811'.6—dc23

                              2013011564

Composed in Dante MT Std 11.5/13.5
Display type is Dante MT Std

Contents

XXX.

Flirt

X.

"Field of Diamonds in the Sky"

Every second, one in eight Americans
looks at the moon and tonight
it has holes in it from all the staring. My elbow
has stopped bleeding but the dull throb
in my back, old friend, has returned. I've stopped
off for the smoothie special, Jamaican
Me Crazy, the taste of dusk. No matter
what's been broken, I've always been amused
when the E.R. says quantify your pain,
one to ten. What to do with
the striations of feeling I can't
enumerate, say that's an eight
o'clock mood. I don't mind
some pain. My wife said the moon
has the best milk for a baby,
go get it. My wife says I love you
but not as much as I would
if you could fly. I'm desired
at a party in this valley tonight
but the things I'd like to taste there
are the difference between fun
and happiness. When I returned
from surfing Teahupo'o, my brother said
you feel more alive in those two
weeks than you do all year
but you've got to work. The body
was meant to take risks, seek
forgiveness not receive permission. With
a baby, sneezing has become fun again
but this Jamaican Me Crazy is a secret,
a little pit stop not in the schedule
between baked chicken
and let's spoon. Depending
on how you fly, it takes two
days to get to the moon. This world
loves comfort but I don't know a body
that doesn't benefit from some pain.

Love & Death

That cliff face where the sandstone

footholds broke under our weight

& the red rocks echoed into

little avalanches & blue sky. Not

until the Bryce Canyon rangers hoisted

us over the cliff's edge did we

look down, where we

started from & almost fell

to, those monolithic boulders

on the canyon floor no bigger

than my red thumbnail

pressed against that sky. In

the emergency lights & bronze

of afternoon, Cristina's face

looks wet & as we drive out

the national forest to find

a diner I ask had she ever

wondered if she had just died

but the person she was with

wanted her back so badly

that they wished her back. Life,

she said, was like that growing up

in El Salvador during the war,

the guerillas or government

attacking at night. Her family

huddled together in the living room

under blankets & automatic fire

& everyone dying & wishing

each other back. Except they

didn't get milkshakes afterward. It was

always around dawn & she'd go

with her father to pick mangoes from the yard

so they could drizzle the fruit's orange

meat with green aiguashte. Or they'd pick

watermelons to be quartered & sprinkled with salt—

tastes so bright they knew they'd survived.

History

The orchids in the flower shop droop in prayer—
a president and his war procession shake
preselected parade hands up the street.

Juan Juan, my barber, asks in Spanish,
these elections, these wars, do I protest?

He says, "I would. Mi corazón está aquí
but I'm not really here."

He sharpens his strop razor.
The sun hits the aluminum windowsill
                                    at full squint.

For months at lunch at the cantina
I've looked at the halved bodies on the front page
and done nothing

but draw zebras with table salt,
make, on my way home,
the neighbor's plastic flamingos chuckle.

"I've protested privately," I say, "but I haven't
joined that peace dance downtown."

Juan Juan puts his razor back against my neck.
"Your hands," he says, "are beautiful."

"They're white eagles
                        with bullet holes through their chests."

Rave On

Those were always good parties

and those were always good cops

that broke us up with batons and night suns

and off we would run to dead-end

canyons with nicknames like "End of the World"

where the city's lights and ocean spun

thousands of feet below us in a perfumed

dizzy of Lucky Lager and mule deer

and sage and bong water. But that

night the party was thrown by a father

for his daughter

because her mother, *his wife*, had taken

her own life. She'd told him when they

met in their twenties she wouldn't

want to live into her forties. The note

she left behind: "I just can't

imagine it. The wrinkles, my body

and friends' bodies—pouched pears—

the failures and excuses." A friend wanted

me to hook up with her, the daughter,

you'd make a good pair, he said

because my mom had already died too

and so I was the expert on loss

but I went home to soothe

in the TV's blue light and Johnny Carson's

mellifluous voice. He was interviewing a young actress,

"What's it like being a new mom?" and her answer

—thin lips any teenager would kiss—"Moist. Life

is incredibly moist" and I now know

she was right. Tonight, our kids are finally

asleep and I'm mopping up the water around the tub.

The breast pump pulls my wife's nipples

impossibly deep into its tubes—

I didn't know they could do that—

with a whoosh, a wince, a giggle.

This life of mine

is no longer mine to take away.

American Thrush

Search and Rescue

I've been thinking about theories
of collective unconsciousness, trying
to will the 11,832-foot peak that
dead ends this valley to move a little
so I can see the meadow behind—mule ear,
dusky horquilla, drought spring—
and the base camp of my late teens. The man-boy
there, above tree line, lightness
of thin air, so thin Carlos, furloughed
from juvie to learn alpine rescue,
rolls into me in his mummy bag, "I haven't
told anyone this yet." "What?" "I stabbed
someone the night before we came out here,
I stabbed them real bad." "Is there
any other way," I asked, "to stab
someone?" and he didn't laugh and I watched
him sleep all starlight and in the morning
we rope-coursed a cliff face to pull a woman
with broken coccyx out of an ice pick shoot,
to replace the adrenaline of guilt
with the adrenaline of risk. Tonight
I want the mountain to shift a little
to the left so I can watch John Muir
walk away from his rigid Protestant
Scot father, so I can watch him
pioneer woods and cliffs, unknown
flora, unknown fauna, at night,
moon, no moon, water oozle, no oozle,
with his dog Stickeen and remember
what it was like not to back down
to fear, to the things that might happen
and the things one "should" do. But
in these ski slope condos without snow,
in the minds of the chickadees, the collective

unconscious is elsewhere tonight. My friend
puts his daughter to bed with a bottle
of milk. Her second word after Cooper, the dog,
was "terrorist," and I can hear someone watching
a documentary on the Ambush at the River of Secrets,
another battle in another War of Secrets. At any moment,
one out of every four people in this country
is concentrating on Jesus showing up
within the year, and I'm giving up
on the mountain to call a friend
who won't get the mail because it could
contain a new flu and then I will
join 5.6 million other Americans watching
their favorite ex-model host a cooking show,
make ceviche and marvel how an old,
overweight fiction writer, 87
million Muslims once wanted to kill,
got to bed her, bravely, every night.

Bay Street

The yellow caution tape cuts through the fog.
The red and blue police lights strobe the fog.

The orange coroners' jackets comb the gray sand.
Her body bag left a shadow in the sand.

~

Mom used to say stay
off the beach at night.
Gangbangers bang
on the beach at night.
Mom didn't know I
drank forties on the beach
at night. That we, Star and me—
there's no pretty way to say it—
fucked fourteen times in the sand
that night. Mom didn't know Star.
I didn't know Star. We met in
the mosh pit for Sonic Youth.
We had too much energy for ska.
Mom was dead then.
One time for each year I was alive.
That, I thought, was being alive.

~

Fucking cholos the witness says.
Poor girl he says.
Fucking cholos took turns.
Line of five under the tower
then gunshots. Ran up
the sand and hopped into a dropped
Caddy & peeled out of the lot. The silence
after. He'd come down the bluff to smoke
a fatty and down an oil can and see

if the swell filled in. Sixteen
he says. She was . . .

~

In the days after me
Star took turns with each of my friends.
My friends took turns with her.
Star wanted to be popular.
My friends made Star popular.
She did not want love & thus
made clear her need for love.

~

The yellow caution tape tied from trash can
to trash can, a type of altar for the detectives
and fingerprint specialists picking up shell
casings, the small offerings left last night
when she resisted. What dawn patrol surfers
see before the beach goers get here. Our
wet suits put on in silence, the cold
water turning our faces blue-white
as we kneel under waves, cheat death,
the only way we know how to honor
the beach dead—   those detectives
kneeling at her side in silence, in prayer.

~

Cool in the tide line where you
feel the onshores but hot on the sand
berm if you stay low. Everything
sparkle and squint and sleepy
at the same time. Small particles
of dust rise into your nose and mouth
each time you dig your hand deep
down where night hides. Once Ghodes

came up with a pair of old diapers.
Patterns of salt had dried into
the peach fuzz on our cheeks. What
to do. Star had moved on to the boys
in the other school. She sat with her
friends who had also moved on to boys
in another school. The girls from our school
wouldn't talk to her. We didn't know Star's
last name. We didn't know
what school she went to. Let's
throw her in one of the boys said.
Good idea we said.

~

There've been others in the sand.
They drive out of the city thinking
a little space and things'll work out
but the horizon just crushes them.
The thirty-something in the tux,
the red carnation still in his black lapel.
The rag man who drank antifreeze
to keep warm. The green foam
bubbled around his indigo lips.
Toxic shock the lifeguard said.
But they did it to themselves.
The way the horizon rises over their
heads from where they lay on shore.

~

August baked sand burns the same
as asphalt in summer. But I
didn't notice. I was holding Star's arm
and she was screaming and laughing.
She landed in the thick bloom
of trash and green algae in the storm
drain pond that stunk from its own stillness.

Her body put the first ripples
in the water since the March
rains. When Star stood strands
of green muck draped her face.
She was laughing. Everyone
was laughing. Our black towels laid
rumpled on the sand in the distance
like empty body bags.
Funny.

~

This swell, a deep-water
ground swell. A set wave
approaches. On shore
the coroner's camera flash
cuts through the fog. The waves
hit the shelf and disappear.
The result of a minor disruption
in the atmosphere. How I wish
I could say this swell is caused
by her death. How I've made her
float over the waves now. We took
our turns. How we gave each other
high fives as if our bodies quivering
in moonlight were an achievement.
How we let the erasure begin.

Astral Tryst

I light the room with a porcelain bowl.
I soak dried mushrooms in the bowl.
I call my boss's wife—
Life is deliberate.

But calling your boss's wife is different than calling your wife—
My boss's wife is named Cinder.
She comes over in a dress like a honeybee.
I open a door that says "My heart is a gaping door."
The mushrooms absorb the night.

From this point on all decisions are accidents
which means they are not decisions at all. She says:
"Did you see the sky? It is constellated with spilled milk."

She says: "If you lay the boss's wife
you age twenty years and your fingers fall off
and your hands look like dried mushrooms."
Did I say my heart was a gaping door?

I add butter, onions, red wine, the mushrooms to an iron skillet.
She lays me down on the floor.
Her skin is stovefire.
The sauce simmers.
Her nipples are comets.
She says, "Love me sparingly and tomorrow,
at work . . . the memory will burn."

At work, I whisper to my coworkers,
"Let us strike. Let us no longer
have things in common
with those afraid of fire."

The Coroner in the Grove

The man's body, his bruises, rotting oranges.

When he returned from the war he wanted to open a thermometer
    museum—
Brass fixtures rescued from nineteenth-century schooners.
Index fingers of mercury measuring up their centers.

But his mother diverted him: "Don't do that!
                        You won't go anywhere!"

                    Where is anywhere?
I grew up with vastness.
I grew up carving oceans into walking sticks
and birds onto those oceans
so I'd have a place to anchor myself as I drifted.
"That's where the Hooded Merganser rests."
But even when etched into ash, birds fly away.

              First lesson: objects are nothing more than wishes.

Before the man went West, his grandfather said:
                  "So much light and freedom out there
                    what else can you do but screw up."
I love that,
  "screw *up*"—
Even our mistakes have direction.

I grew up too quickly to study awe.
              As if there was "somewhere" to get to—

His skin, dissolving orange skin.
His skin, bruised dusk.

My Uncle's Three Thousand Photographs of Point Dume

What, after his wife passed, did he take
from the four rolls of one seal framed
wide angle against the horizon,
its head lost to the surf?

Why the rolls of the seal's neck,
its tendons' variety of violets and magentas
cauterized by salt and the right aperture?
Why must I introspect good lighting.

The sea cucumber pink and big as his forearm
clouding a tide pool in this series labeled Dioxazine Purple?
and then gone. In its ink.
In his light.

Eighteen carousels of slides
sitting edited in his chest for how many years
before me, in this projector-glow?
What does the sea air restore to a blank stare?

What, in the months after someone passes, do forty
frames of a cormorant give, feathers ruffled into fox bait,
then body bloated, then eye missing,
then skeletal?

Nothing Here Really Happened but Everything Here Is True

That fat band-tailed pigeon perched on the wire between my ears. Mosquito abatement stream covered in eucalyptus dusk. Dear Go Getter, that musk you've taken with you. That hand on the swing that would fit inside my hand. In that pigeon's eye: a mother sneaks a smoke behind the ivy bunker, that small c growth gently emerging on the part of her brain that once governed love. The Opal's engine still warm in the driveway and talk of a Le Car that won't go far. In that pigeon's eye: a father fries kosher bacon and I'm feeling coyote. Photo lesson #2: go to the carport, shut the sun out with sheets. Light it. Cut bell pepper down through shoulder to placenta rough. Photo Lesson #4: light it. Teach me contrast between contrasts, seed and skin, Rauschenbergy symmetry of endocarp cells, primary colors sharpen in black and white. Red, green, yellow but no one is ready for the blues. What do you need to know? Your mom's father. He once stole a neighbor's Great Dane and gave it to her as a birthday present. So? In that pigeon's eye: A father makes a promise he can keep: Everything in this world makes sense eventually. Except for the things that don't. Dear Sinister Kid: Answers are things you forget. That hollow under honeysuckle overgrowth. That glass pipe next to Wendy Flatz as she lies down for you to taste the cool contours of loss. Dear Night Jasmine, the chicken blood on the side of the house from the moonlight raccoon. Dear Pacific blue jay feeding from that boy's chromatic white hand. Dear Blackberries in dragonfly hum heat. This is the Fibonacci dizzy of the world's making. Gift and curse. What rises. Sage and sage. Deer and dears.

How I Made My Money

I went to the loon and swapped

a "hello" for its mournful

song. I went to the barn and exchanged

a fistful of wasps for a swallow's iridescence.

I sold letters of absolution as Christmas

gifts to the Lehman brothers. I made

my money the old-fashioned way—I told

a bull one thing and a bear another. I executed

iron butterflies and short straddled

the black-crowned Phoebe's pessimistic

black skull. No photo of me can be taken

without a price. When twelve hundred and fifty

blackbirds fell from the sky in a small

Midwest town, I shorted avian futures. Dawn

was a gray mist and the red stripes

on those birds' black wings

cut through the steam of Omaha's

coffee cups. I got out of the market

on a Fibonacci sunflower sequence high

and bought back in on a cheetah spot sequence low.

I am the new soul of this country.

Go long on the cloud.

A Coming of Age Story Part II

Two bottles remain upright, filled with green sunlight,
against the chain link that separates the patients
on the State Suicide Watch from my brother
and me. Broken bottles are two points. Knockdowns,
nothing. We are waiting for our parents—the weight
of the baseball feels good in my hand. Something solid
I can throw. Something I understand. Shards sparkle
on the blacktop like small clumps of sea grass.
The patients come to the fence to watch
our game. There's joy in those shards,
I think. They're collecting them the way
we collect smoothed beach glass. "You
of all people should know better"
the director will scream at my father
but now the patient who smiled
at us most is sitting down in a corner. He whispers,
"Thank you." He's still in his pajamas
but his arm is turning red.

Tease

The Eucalyptus trees mottle the sunlight

and you are taking the curls from my hair

and weaving them into braids, into baby

dreads. The SteelPulseMinorThreatDreamSyndicate

mix I made you bass the neighborhood

and we share a couple of Mickey's

Big Mouths to quiet the reverb of desire

that hums between us. You're taking

the surf out, the boy who cried

shark before the news cameras came

out and teasing me into the life of cool.

Strand by strand you ran your hands

through my hair, weaving it

through an afternoon, through six

jobs, two universities, into the evening

I walked home holding another Jennifer's

hand on the edge of Oakland (Cokeland

we called it) and I got cold cocked

by brass knuckles for twenty bucks and being

a "dreadlocked white boy." I shaved

my head as soon as I could see and talk again

but what you teased into me, this desire

for art, this desire for closeness, hasn't left.

I'm rehabbing a torn shoulder at the YMCA pool

near our teenage homes. (Basketball

in the park for money again . . .) Old Russian

Jewish couples are doing watercise

and the sun feathers through the water.

I can't help but watch their large, varicose

thighs shake each time they jump. Jennifer,

that afternoon, that was intimacy

before we knew it, what some couples trade

for sex, trade for desires hollowing out.

XX.

Your Baby Ain't Sweet Like Mine

Sometimes fall arrives & you turn thirty-something
& are diagnosed with a seventy-year-old's disease,
which you shrug off with a martini & quip
from your fiancée "honey, you've always been
a bit quick" which is Ha Ha funny but smarts
the way the receiving end of wit always smarts
so you go Buddhist again but neglect to give up
all desire & settle for the bit about embracing
suffering, which the sudden absence of friends
suggests isn't working out so well. Sometimes
in your fears of being hurt—the truck on the freeway
with the pipe protruding stopping short & the pipe
through your windshield—you become Woody
Allenish & your father says Woody is okay funny
on screen but a pain in the ass to hang out with
so you get back to the business of creating hope
& eat plenty of fiber & drink lots of water & after
years of waiting for no real reason you landscape
the backyard for the wedding & make new friends
who come over to discuss sustainable softscape,
your new love for the coneflower, aka Echinacea,
the way its thistly orb center projects skyward
& its petals fall away, a purple badminton bird,
determined & lovely. Sometimes June Gloom stretches
into August & you get married in July & people
take the lychees out of their martinis & put them in
their eye sockets & dance the rumba & you scoot off
to Italy where you go to more churches in a week
than your agnostic blood has been in a lifetime
& marvel over shaved pecorino on sliced pear
S drizzled with sunflower honey
& return home with a micro-perforation
in your colon & spend a week in the hospital
& surgery becomes imminent but there's
an eighty-something percent chance you'll
survive so together you throw a party entitled

The Last Supper & project film noir onto
the back of your house so that your last
memory before you're cut is of food & friends
stilled on blankets & wrapped in the muslin of dusk
& sometimes you wake at 5:22 in the morning
& it's winter again & you sit on the edge
of the bed & trace a new scar down the center
of your belly & your new wife sits up
next to you & asks with the emergency room
still in her voice, "Honey?"

Shahid

Everyone, you said, looks so lovely in Glenfiddich land.
When you leave, how will this not be a ghost land?

"Surfers in the Northeast are the same as Bengal tigers in the West."
I drove across country to be an exotic in the Beloved's land.

Your scotch and gold silk, that dark bar's only flame.
The punkers watched you, a mystic in their tired land.

In a heart chamber I store his souvenirs from evanescence.
Curry hot & masala fragrant, let me guide you to Shahid's land.

Your absence, always a presence. I'm making a vindaloo,
an offering, to bring the angel back to his abandoned land.

In your "Farewell" "my memory gets in the way of our history."
The poets still gather lines to keep you in our scriptured land.

Do Kashmir and the Koran keep you with us tonight?
If it helps, I will, for a night, believe in your God land.

In the future I only speak of you in the future.
His skin will be saffron in the promised land.

As a ghost in the snow I will come to you in the snow.
"Noah," you will say, "be the Mojave of this cold land."

When You Burn You Become Euphoric

Water, the way it burns after carne asada
with too much tapatío. The way
your sinuses clear so that the men and women
in this hotel bar drinking blue
drinks in plastic cups, line dancing
to country rap, make emotional sense.
When you drive all day your body
goes numb & your mind wanders places
you wish it wouldn't & tapatío in an
interstate bar brings you back. When
you burn, burn victims say (heat
hot enough to melt asphalt) your
body, having crossed through pain,
grants euphoria, what's left after
prick & cut, loss & sadness, the smushed
crabgrass in your daughter's backyard
this morning as you moved her out
of that house. The way she whispers
to your wife in the room now. Let him
keep his house. The way his house
would burn if lit. The way these drinks
numb you up after the tapatío
makes you feel again. Burn survivors say
there is nothing like your skin coming
back because you feel every thing
at once, total presence, no thing
worse. How your daughter would say
euphoria, even if it is a false state, is too
good for him. How you say let him
be. The disco ball makes
the fat lady's eyes twinkle ember orange
as she slaps Mr. CharcoalButtonDown
on his butt. What we really want
is to be half in this world
at all times. We say breaking up
because when you take away the "S"

from sex you drag yourself through
all that went wrong with Ex,
that disintegration. That
dance move, the guy
next to you says, is a tortilla cross
and asks "how you'd like to get
crossed up with her?" and laughs.
Pun & chuckle. This firelight
bass lounge. This night, one long
electric slide.

American Thrush

"I Want to Do Right but Not Right Now"

I've made a coat out of the stars, tucked

ursa minor in close to my heart, zipped

the huntress out, her lips away from my lips—

I'm thinking now, wife, lover after sixteen years still

and never still, our kids, always, kids—"fingers, thumbs,

monkeys hum, monkeys beating on a drum . . ."

      The woman in the bar, her eyes, blue stars,

that spot where neck meets clavicle, a milky way

to rest lonelinesses. "You look stiff,"

she said and so, story: My back blew out.

Malibu. Surfing. An aerial. Above a wave,

that thin air, corkscrewed into an eighteen-

year-old's idea of fun. (I love that, "blown

out." How breath shifts bone.) She gravitated

closer to me. I forget I always flirt

before I think. I forget to spin

back to what really happened, the whole

story: that disc shifted above whitewater

but did not rupture from its opaque fluid dream,

bathed the femoral nerve in spinal acid, until

I was pushing a stroller up Hill Street. I forget

how desire constellates every bar and that each

glass of vodka, backlit, ice clink and glimmer,

are falling stars. All those years before I had my dears, spent

in devout study of cocktail and innuendo

(in your end? Oh! . . . Sweet puberty!)

but no one ever said much about Rilke,

compatible solitude, the silences that define

intimacy and how much pressure those

silences bare when sex gets muddled

into work and kids, schedules and money,

the slippery plastic gears of middle-class being. What

body doesn't want wanting. What mind doesn't

want to be left alone. I don't want to talk

about the reasons I don't want to talk

about the reasons I don't want to talk.

But if I speak only in the words of other men . . . Oh wife,

my ursa major, big bear, polaris, white, no

yellow, over crystal peak, my way home—

am I thinking clearly now?—you are my

Synchilla, my polyester down fill tonight. Kids,

great little bears, breast pockets, you make me

look good, next to me, away from me,

where the gods and demigods have set you

tonight, where Ptolemy first found you,

that Sky Meadow. There the water ouzel

lives, bluish gray, aka water thrush. It thrives

in those high altitudes year round, never

gets cold, has three eyelids, a nictitating

membrane so it can see under water,

as it dives and hunts in rapids.

Flirt

"We need to aspirate your testicle," the urologist says

and I confess that I've had many aspirations

but that is not one of them and so I go home

to calculate my carbon footprint and read

an article my wife left for me on fruit

bats and the revelation they're the only

other mammals to engage in oral sex,

something I should still be interested in

even if she's busy at work. Life is funny

even when it's not, I'm trying

to remember that. There's talk of mudslides,

of debris flows that'll wipe out entire cul-de-sacs

but the sky is still clear. I admire people

who can plan this life. When I dropped off

my daughter at preschool the thin blonde

said, "My husband's a beast, we should go

for a cocktail, he'll never know." All that effort

in my late teens and twenties to "hook up"

and "hang out." No one ever said anything

about hanging on to what you have. Without

love I am a noisy going, a clanging symbol. "Maybe

some other time," I said and listened to the talk

on the radio about happiness, on who gets to define

what it means to be happy and whether or not

so much talk about being happy just makes us sad.

For once in my life I wasn't thinking

about what a doctor would think

but just about grace and aging, the patient

to the nurse after the transplant, "I may be eighty

but watch out, my heart is only twenty-two." All this talk

about pathology, what happened and who

is responsible, no, liable for us being

and so little about this moment

and the one after. The coastal succulents

cast crab leg shadows on the beach wall and there's

a dolphin cloud in the sky. The kids will want

to play Neptune when they get home

but I still have time for to run. This is fun.

Instructions for Checking the Surf at Scorpion Bay

Drive past the sewage plant north of K28 & through
the trucking station on the dirt road & ignore
the eyes of the drivers back from their pothole rambles
down to Ensenada or up to Tijuana as they look
at your surfboards & mutter *gringo* or *pendejo*
or both. Keep your windows rolled up & look straight
as you slow over the bump by the guard tower & head out
to the bluff where a few families sit in the sand
cooking hermit crabs or mussels discolored
by the stinking water. Resist wanting to help
them in some way & resist admonishing yourself
for thinking you could help them or they would want
your help. If it is a day in late March, after a storm,
the clouds that make the water look ominous, like a warning,
are a warning. Pay attention. Does the sun
glisten out from behind those clouds & tinfoil
across the whitecaps & highlight waves
randomly filling up the channel with closeouts & whitewash
that stings your eardrums & sticks to your hair long after
you've showered & swallowed a shot of mezcal
with the worm? Is there a strong current sweeping south
along the inshore holes towards the sewage plant?
If you are desperate to paddle out,
find the riptide by the drainpipe & let it
carry you into the line up
but get out of it before you end up
in a shipping lane. If you just became old enough
to have had your first proposition
from a shadow in an Ensenada bar
then you are sitting at this overlook
with your brother's best friend
& want to say something clever
if the wind just stops & the tide goes
down & the swell changes direction
we could have a good time. Resist
or he will wish you were your brother. Plan

ahead. Bring two Negra Modelos so you can open them
in the door latch & not have to say anything
but can sit there & think of a story you read in middle school
now distant enough to be comforting. Be thankful
the heater has kicked on & the bubbles in your beer
make small pops when they rise. Be thankful
your brother has a friend with enough sense
not to paddle out in soup. But when
you begin to think how lucky you are
you have not been hassled this trip,
do not follow your brother's friend's stare
up the road to the federale with an M16
pointed between you & the ground.
Tan suit & epaulets & bayonet
in front of you, but it is not your fault. From this point on
embrace silence & go along
with this federale as he spreads you out
on the hood. Do not test your Spanish & do not
watch as he lights your last cigarette & licks his finger,
dark & glistening in that sun out from behind those clouds,
& wipes his finger along the foil
inside the cigarette package & puts
his finger back in his mouth to taste
if you've been doing lines. Don't do lines.
Resist looking at your brother's best friend
for reassurance & don't say anything
other than your name as he takes out
a napkin & pen from his breast pocket
& goes looking for a stash in the glove
compartment & under the front seats
& pulls up the back seat & flips
through the dive book & stops
in the first aid section & laughs
at the two pink men giving each other
mouth to mouth & drops the manual
in the dirt. This is crucial: be happy
your brother's best friend
stole your first girlfriend & keeps

pictures of them in bed together
in his car. The federale has let
his rifle dangle from his shoulder
to look at the photos &
test your brother's friend
"Es tu novia?"
Do not do anything, do not think the surf
has gotten better, do not think of your beer,
the way the brown bottle holds the sun,
what photographers call the golden hour,
until the federale smiles & your brother's friend smiles
"Ella es muy bonita.
You can go."

Omens

You twist your pinky into the buckshot
hole of a rock dove's breast and touch
its heart, little plumb seed. Emily's
sequestered herself by the lean-to.
In the MSR's light, her hands
are blue flame. A lie's nothing
more than a little desire gone
wrong. The sun going down is as red
as the desert stretched out between you
and the highway. Another woman waves
on the blacktop. Her mouth moves
but she's too far away to have a voice. Her ring
catches the sun, blinks like a hazard light.

There's No Reason to Be Weird

"It's fucking gorgeous today," the guy

outside the bagel place says and I've

not much to complain about either. Since

the K9 unit took the guy in the neighbor's

garage away, they've turned the all day

party down to a dull hum. Their dog

hasn't even bit anyone for a couple

of weeks. Today I'm forgiving myself

for everything I haven't done. Not

everything needs to add up. Such freedom. I will

stop by the kosher Chinese and order brown

rice with egg whites. Go a little crazy

and order a Coke with extra carbs. Go a little crazier,

stop worrying about swallowing fistfuls

of razorblades. The shrink—there's always

a shrink!—said we're full of ego-dystonic

and ego-syntonic thoughts. For me, giving

the neighbor's dog a fistful of peanut butter

with downers would be ego-dystonic, although not

completely a bad idea. But I'm taking the day off

from shrinks. For this I will have to apologize. The black

hooded Phoebe waits on the golden bamboo

to execute bees. A large dirt hole is a grave

unless it is filled with water, then it is a pond.

Today I might even finish digging. Tomorrow

I might even have a pond.

Ocean Park #79

Agua Dulce's on fire & I'm rushing home
to save my pets or I'm dreaming. These mornings
I wake in what locals call June Gloom—
which means I don't wake at all. I don't
know. June Gloom, a fog without a fog's smoke
effect so I can still see Keenan & his wife,
their children already at surf camp, snap
towels at each other, their bodies cream-colored
& worn as old terrycloth. These mornings
I get up & put on my three-piece suit
with hundreds of eggs attached
(yolks drained, shells intact) & go
into my backyard to feed my duckbilled
platypus scallops. What the conceptual artist
conceptualized when he designed my suit
I don't know. I just like how the eggs
cut through June Gloom's warm mist
like tiny headlights, this warm mist that glazes me,
glazes everything into early afternoon
like the hangovers of strange dreams.
In between shellfish I let my platypus suckle
my pinky, cradling him so as not to break an egg,
so as not to touch the poisonous spurs
on the heels of his hind legs & get stung
further into coma. In the realm of celestial
jokes, June Gloom is a one-liner, but the gods
in the corner of that billion-year-old bar
still cackle over the platypus. "Get this,"
one of them says, "how 'bout a spoon-billed,
beaver-tailed, web-footed, electromagnetically
sensitive mud-digging egg-laying mammal
whose spurs scientists will think
are for sexual combat?" I have never
engaged in sexual combat, an all-out war
with spur & shield & fur in a mud burrow
but I empathize with the jokes of minor gods. In this non-fog,

this haze between seasons, between consciousnesses,
I want to reach out to the blue starfish,
most poisonous of all echinoderms, constantly
rising to the lagoon's surface, lonely in its
cloak of poison, to hold it lovingly, turquoise
in my white hand. My neighbors, now drinking coffee
on their front porch, look at me
like an anomaly, monsoon season
in the desert, their faces disconcerting
as June Gloom, wrinkled as horror.
I say "hello" & they look at me
as if a chicken hawk, its beak the size of my
middle finger, circled overhead
as if I were wearing a suit made of eggs.

Amber & Embers

It was too soon
to think of her passing,
so I passed
evenings in the water.

I wanted to look
like a boy out for a surf,
go from a boy
to a shadow

against the pasteled horizon
and from a shadow
to being the sun, a part of the sun
as it slipped over the other side.

I was happy enough,
on clear days,
to float
and see a "bottom" underneath me.

I forgot
waves.
I forgot
the shore.

Sand shifted in the undercurrent
along the bottom and,
as the sun got lower,
clear water turned

into the purples and oranges of reflection
and my wet suit
became a part
of that reflection.

As the sky went black, slowly,
the water went black,
slowly, and I lost sight
of my feet.

I lost sense
of what moved beneath me,
I lost track
of what swelled towards me.

Decisions by instinct.
That was fear.

Cold water, sitting on the edge of light,
the willful deprivation of sense—

my Baptist friend says
"You were trying to cross over,
to get as close to her as you could
without leaving entirely."

On shore, shadows
sifting through trash cans,
the sound of Santa Ana winds drying leaves,
bring you back.

On shore, I changed quickly:
stripped my wet suit into puddles
of headlights on the side of highway,
shook out the salt water from my inner ear.

The Cruelest Jokes Have No Punch Lines

The yellow kangaroo paw dulled by dark
and the neighbor's pterodactyl child
off to bed with *The Wild Things*
and Maria's cocooned in the house
burying the baby she delivered today
not moving because it happens
for no other reason than it happens
by reading an article about a diver
tangled up with a dead body at 907 feet
the dive computer on his wrist flashing red
the nitrogen levels in his blood like drinking
six dry martinis back to back
so now she's displacing one body
with another body the same article I read
earlier with my martini on the roof deck
to get the alcohol the sunset the article
one body to displace another body
to displace the one-armed man-child
sent from the pet crematorium to carry
my eighty-pounds dog up flights of stairs
to an orange flamed flatbed
grab him by the legs he said
he's going to start to leak

East Bay

There's nothing like a good fire
to cook s'mores with family
and keep the creek skunk away
unless it's a neighborhood you love
that's burning and the smoke's eclipsed the sun
and cast the bay in orange haze
and we go to the top of the astronomy building
to get closer to the smoldering
and all night the ash flakes
over our cars our sidewalks our lives

&

in the morning no cars come down
Claremont Blvd. and Dave and I duck
the yellow caution tape and ride
the same steep hill we always ride
from Alvarado to the ridge the asphalt's melted
and the Green and Green craftsmen we loved
have cindered down to their skeletons
except for one door frame holding
a smoky view of that bay
and that story of the father we couldn't rescue
who jumped into the Jacuzzi to escape the flames
and boiled alive

&

that William James quote I held onto then
about anyone who's ever looked upon the face of a dead parent
must realize the fact that matter
took on such a precious form
should make all matter sacred ever after—
comes back to me now
as Danielle makes cocoa
as Simone sleeps in her baby seat
as the marshmallows on the campfire sticks
orange and blacken.

Somewhere North of Here Picasso Painted Something

The guidebook says the countryside
is covered in every shade of verdure
but forgot to mention the ocean and sky
covered in every shade of slate. I'd say verdure
too if I wrote guidebooks but where
we are going we are not going to decide,
which is why we're still here. Some things
come naturally and thus cause
the most pain. The truth
is gray slate and blue slate. The fishermen
in the harbor never lie
until you talk to them
but on mornings with weather like this
there's not much to say. On afternoons
after a day of lifting heavy Scintilla wine
and swaying like their masts in weather,
they talk. What Yeats learned
from the mystics in Los Angeles
was perception. Everyone was very nice to us
there. They all had answers
until I listened and I listened carefully
to everyone. This morning we started out
in front of a lovely garden with rose bushes,
walked five hundred meters on one road
and five hundred more on another,
and came to a lovely garden with roses. Note
to self: try one road. Wilky said perception
is wonderful but useless without action. Note
to wife and future child: this time let's try settling
in a farmhouse over a sun struck break
and grill the catch of the day
over bowls of happy. You know
I keep my promises as well as the weather
and this time thunder won't touch us.

Giovanna

There is the you before me on accident in this office of Eames and polished concrete and the you I remember last standing with me nineteen years ago in front of my mirror, both of us naked. Your skin the color of pale tangerines, how I had imagined it since the swoosh insignia on my sneakers made me run faster through the years you went out with my friends and I breathed in the chalk dust through my nose in dull high school classrooms so as not to pay attention to you, your scent. And how I've carried around that moment since our second year in that little junior college. You coming up to my shack in Topanga on New Year's Eve to drink mezcal and Chambord. That moment we kissed, how I thought you'd shove me away and that moment after, studying each other's bodies. Your legs, impossibly thin, the scars on my knees from laying down my motorcycle on Deadman's Curve, the small of your back—I thought I could cozy there for years. "Look," you said, "how well our bodies fit together," and I was terrified.

There is the you before me in this office and the you I was last with sixteen years ago, standing in front of the mirror, our skin the color of tangelos.

Your hair was black and straight to the small of your back, that cleft, I thought I'd bliss there for years. But "look," you said,

"how our bodies fit together perfectly," and I was terrified. The way I heard it, prophetic, as if being together was not a choice and the next day

I broke it off. Your stepfather, your last parent, was dying as my mom just had and I couldn't explain it but knew I couldn't be trusted with someone

else's loss. "I've found syringes," your roommate said in front of the library two weeks later. "No," I said, "there was nothing I could do," and thought the needle

took you. I embalmed guilt in memory's salt water and practiced forgetting. Love, I didn't know, has more to do with timing than anything. "Yes," I say. "I'm married."

A Coleridge Shark Dog Good-bye Song

         Morning moon over sierras:
opaque, the thinned edge of last season's snow
on summer granite. That fading. I want wonder
to wake me so I tap on the "news," a video
that's gone viral: two dogs, reef-colored, swim and bark
in a shallow bay, five silhouettes below them—
bull sharks. The dogs are gleeful if dogs can fill
with glee and so I watch the dogs herd the sharks,
the sharks comply like sheep, swim
deeper into the shallows until one strays
and the dog dives and bites the shark.

In the 70s, after *Jaws* came out, I wouldn't
swim in any water at night for fear a great white
would break through the drain and devour me.
Every adult I know near middle age hums
dudut dudut, dudut dudut, when confronted
with swimming in large bodies of water. After
the movie's release it became cool
in a Hemingway-I-have-more-chest-hair-than-you
way to hunt great whites and hang shirtless
photos of yourself in your office, the bloody
fish dangling by its tail from a winch, a rod
or a shotgun or a beer in your hands.
But that movie was based on a series of attacks
on the Jersey Shore in 1916, now thought to be
the work of one bull shark too hungry to realize
it would change the entire future of its species.
Before the news of those attacks, before the movie,
sharks were thought to be harmless and while
I know people who know people who've been
attacked, the times surfing I've paddled into
them—eight-foot juvenile white at San Elijo,
grayish silhouette in deeper blue—
I've stilled. I've watched them streamline, slowly,
away from me, no threat—a danger trance.

These are the last unscheduled hours I have
to lounge in the next scheduled years. It was
Sunday and spring when I arrived and today
it is Saturday and summer. The cereal box
is empty, the Earl Grey, gone. Soon my wife will greet me
in the exhaust fluorescent light bright hustle of LAX.
August, my soon to be three-year-old son, his big sister,
Siena, their stuffed dogs, "red and pink red and pink pink,"
under their arms. I took both of them surfing at eleven
months and they've both seen me leave the water
because of a fin in a bait ball and are terrified.
I need to teach them terror lives behind the rib cage
like a small flute and that if they memorize great songs
they can turn that flute into something more like
a kazoo. I need to teach them wafer moon
over Saddle Peak, silhouette shark skulk—
the gospel from the book of wonder that doesn't end.

Main St.

Around you, this café light, reflected

copper & inside the coach ordering

vegan chocolate cake for his girls.

On the news, spilled across the freeway's

blackphalt, a shipment of hot pink sneakers

and here someone's ex is late

& up the street the volleyball

team waits in flip-flops in a gym.

A man rollerblades by

dark & shirtless & native with two

Galapagos iguanas on his head—

everything is as it was before you left.

But nobody's the same since

Black Jack jumped off Borofsky's two-story

ceramic clown last month.

But nobody's different.

"Thank you. She's nine months,"

the mother says to the dog lady.

"And your golden, is she friendly?"

"Yes! She . . . Oh, Butterscotch!

We don't lick baby's toes!

No we don't! Sorry about that."

It's your best friend's ex who's late.

Why four years in the North's ice

apprenticing to a stoic—what she

would give now to have not been afraid

of what she needed then & to have needed less. Three

of the girls from the volleyball team ditched

& got henna tattoos down at Body Paint. It's good

to be home. I'm working on a formula

to slow life down. The girls are trying on

a street vendor's rings. The ex wonders about

your best friend. How some accept & forget & go on.

"They're so young," you say about those girls,

"but their hands are so grown up." "Yes,"

the ex says, "but those fingers will never wear wedding rings.

They look lovely."

Holoholo

I'm looking at the tree outside my window bright green
in this new season of hot rain and thinking *pretty*

& I'm hoping a bluebird will land so I can think *prettier*
& when none does when nothing lands I start to look for a good time

I go back twenty years and hop into my first jalopy
& I'm driving around the big houses up on Capri until I get tired

& pull over to wait for a friend to wait for the night to begin
I sit on the curb figuring out the puzzle on the bottom of my beer cap

& make up a story about that house shaped like a ship
the young widow who lives there just unbuttoned

the sailor she hires twice a week "to ease my suffering," she says
& my beer cap puzzle says something about love

& any minute my date will come to me
in a dress made for tequila shots

but then those cop cars pull up on each side of me again
pin me
          beer in headlights

but this time I don't resist their search
          my seizure

I move slowly almost lethargically
                              as they lay me down
                              nose to pavement
                              finger my pockets for possible
                                   convictions

I tell myself the sprinklers
                    how they continue to turn on up and down the block

obey the drought laws and water after sundown
                    even as I lay here
                                        are a kind of funny

I tell myself "seeing is forgetting the thing one sees"
                                        those cruiser lights they're beautiful

the way they flash and reflect
numinously up the wet pavement
                                into the corners of my eyes

Exploding Ghazal

Your heart in my hand is a bomb tonight.
I'll do what I can if there's a bomb tonight.

News of an explosion. Was your SEAL
brother in a van with a bomb tonight?

A cherry falls through a Manhattan—
the businessman's bomb tonight.

On the bar TV: Green Beret? The Taliban?
I hope the band's the bomb tonight.

And this street is lined with real estate signs.
We've entered a neighborhood of F-bombs tonight.

An Ansel Adams lake. A ridgeline of splendor . . .
But your breasts are the infant's balm tonight.

The paramedic lights in the fog of a neighbor's home.
A kerosene boy, a father's drunk bomb tonight.

The tank toy breaks. A wax soldier's wounded.
My son's face, a moon bomb tonight.

Today, an unidentified missile exploded off Catalina.
Dear Pacific, your sun sets like a bomb tonight.

Marines are training bird drones to land on cacti.
Oh, Noah, do you feel the anxiety bomb tonight?

Suburban

Craig and Joey's dogs are large
so they leave their windows
open for stars to fall
through and fill their dreams
with the purples and yellows of Saturn's rings
and the intangible shades of rest.

On mornings like this one,
when the mowers and smell of cut
grass from the golf course wake them,
they rise and check the sky for clouds,
for the winter stars
faint as dew on the fairways.

They rise and stretch and poke
their heads out the second-story
window and their dogs look up at them
from their body-nests and yawn.

They have had a long night, these dogs,
checking for the people their masters worry about,
men and women from the side of the five par
cops call Dogtown

climbing through their windows
with knives and the efficiency of black cats.
Every couple of hours the sprinklers
tssst tssted, tssst tssst tsssted

and the dogs woke and squiggled
on their backs to rub out fleas,
gathered themselves and perimetered the yard,
stopped and sniffed and peered

through the knocked out
knot hole in the fence,

barked a few times
to affirm their presence.

Not until they listened
for snoring a second time,
the tsssst, tsssssss dripping off,
did they whisper to themselves

"good boy," "good girl,"
back to sleep.

Flea

The new owners unroll their carpet of gold
shag before me, their field of late fall
corn, of wheat, of Russian Tumbleweed, of dried
witch's hair (convolvulaceae). I am this house's
first flea brought in by the new hound,
this house's first domestic gazelle,
obsidian antelope, ebony kangaroo,
beauty's shadow sent by gods
to rule over dust mites, to populate
this carpet, this plain & tundra, with blood
suckers, vectors, cathedrals of sloughed
skin. I am prince of Red Welt, overlord
of Minutiae, the itch tonight
next to the husband's belly button
(the trailhead to the treasure trail)
as his wife goes down on him
in celebration of date night, of ownership,
in celebration of their new home.

Bass Lake

The evening cast in poppy light and our car
dipping in and out of redwood shadow
and the trail dust on our legs feels good
and the dried sweat on the backs of our necks feels good
and the smell of lake and the tiredness behind our eyes
is good. That was farther than any of us
walked in years. Cristina and Forrest hated
me for dragging them up the long hill
in the sun but it was good. We leaned our necks over
the cliff to look for people specks on the beach,
to look at the surf, to look at the sandbars
making the surf, the islands, the whales migrating
through the red triangle, the story of the great
white off the Farallon getting tossed into the
air by a whale repeatedly. No one jumped or fell,
which is good. When I drove these curves last
the girl I was with put her head in my lap to nap
and the cop who pulled me over took me
behind my truck and asked with a wink
what was she doing with her head
in my lap. We had devoured wine and swung
from a rope swing and because I thought
it a good idea to watch my feet break water
when falling two stories
I chipped a front tooth and the blood
in my mouth made the cop nod and let
us go. The baby has started to cry
and we've begun to sing "Ode to Joy" because
lullabies make us cry too and some crying
is good. Cristina and Forrest had looked
at the rope swing and the wood spike
I swung over to reach the water
and questioned my noodle
and stopped me from following
a bobcat into the scotch broom by saying
"father," which means I need to choose

my bobcats more carefully now. *Striden,*
Striden, and the Si Si is falling asleep,
which means she feels good
which means we feel good
which means everything in our world
at this moment is good.

XXX.

For . . .

"And when you kneel in madness your knees are glass,
And so you must stand up again with great care."

~   ~   ~

There were the brass knuckles
that broke the bone that holds my eye

& the times the cops' blue lights pinned me down
with shotguns after someone got stabbed at a party

& the left on an Italian gurney, near septic, prepped to pass
the surgeries that noodling in the intestine's purple loom

& the boy stilled in the pre-calculus of sex
my mom about to slip through my CPR hands

& these violences, a tremor music
you never silence completely.

~   ~   ~

My wife's El Salvador, during the war, before her family was put

on the government's blacklist to be executed. She snuck out of

school with her friends to see a rumor. A boy they knew, his brother

had joined the rebels, so the government troops had stacked him,

dismembered, on his mother's porch, matchstick style, feet and

calves on the bottom, his penis between his hands and under his chin.

His eyelids pinned open so that the town would stare and would be warned. The story is that they hacked him apart while alive, while the local lieutenant fucked a whore in the background, while boy soldiers chewed cocoa leaves.

~ ~ ~

There is that point in hypothermia, just before you die,

when the body feels hot, as if it were on fire,

and you take off all your clothes. I imagine there was a point

when that boy stopped feeling, he could see his limbs, the blood

on whitewashed adobe walls, but pain was replaced

with disbelief. Madness is sometimes defined as a state

separate from the action occurring. In the months that followed,

his mother started to talk in her son's voice and was found

with her hand in a stove's flame, her hand beginning to catch fire,

her hand . . . she felt nothing.

~ ~ ~

Eleven years after the war. Med school. Anatomy. When students get into working with cadavers, the last parts they dissect: feet, hands, the face. Otherwise, too much. Too fast. Overwhelming. The end of the semester. A car crash victim. Hispanic pink feet. We were at dinner. Turkey burgers with soy and ginger, medium rare. Finger fries. "I have a story to tell you," you said. Some school girls. A teenage boy. A mother. Soldiers.

A rumor . . .

An asshole—purple sea anemone. Fine.   But there are some stories so horrific they should not be made beautiful for retelling in poems. They should never be retold and yet they should never be forgotten. My wife doesn't talk about the war, yet I know it lives inside her, a vapor, imperceptible, some breaths shorter than others. Some breaths. Short.

A man with a machete in the Sierra Laguna. Those mountains and that bucket of blood. A boy soldier with an M16. A boy, an M16. The jungles of Nicaragua. Us, traveling. Siena, August, our babies, asleep. Traveling. Two places. Two times. Dirt roads. Rivers. Ghosts from your childhood. Ghosts. Don't stop, you said. No matter what (gun shot)—Don't stop.

We'd been dating, figuring out the each of the other, if we had a place in this world. I smelled of last night's last girl's gardenias and my stomach rumbled with the amoeba I picked up in that Baja bar. You gave me a pill that made my mouth taste of metal. Blood and metal. "I'm comfortable with automatic weapons," you said. Don't forget it.

Healing. The disc in my back shifted
through the femoral nerve and those weeks
after, feeling coming back. In that shower,
steam heat rising, half my body,
snowdrift cold. Heat around me

and cold inside of me, but my life,
this time, was not threatened. Reaction
proportionate to the action. I was not

Gumbied across a sidewalk next to People's Park,
brass knuckles and steel toes, "white fucking rasta,"
dude's taking my girlfriend's purse, and then

younger, still, a mother's life through my fingertips,
no life through my fingertips, I was
present, never   so present.

I was nowhere near
that stratosphere
of that boy, that mother.

Yet I wonder where the ghosts live
in my wife, why I twist still, at conflict's edge.
How will our children internalize our violences,
will they remain distant from them,
snow gathering in the blind eyes of statues,
their hands, steel, stainless, over this page?

~   ~   ~

Outside my window, a small patch of grass
wakes between granite. High-altitude
meadow. Boys from wrestling camp,
girls from dance camp on a gondola
to swim in a mountaintop resort pool,
to swim in the dizzy of first transgressions.
This is a prayer for them. This is a prayer
for my children asleep in their bunk beds
at sea level. May they never acquire
death's thin cello wire,
what connects my cortex to my toes, what plays
memory's midnight wrong song. This is
a prayer for Nostalgia and Innocence, those
lovers, their sfumato edges, their downy
corners. There is beautiful music
out there. There is beautiful music.

NOTES

"Field of Diamonds in the Sky": The poem, although it does not have much to do with the song, takes its title from Johnny Cash's "Field of Diamonds."

"Rave On": The title is owed to Buddy Holly's song, which is great in and of itself but so is the version M. Ward did, which I was listening to at the time.

"American Thrush": The water ouzel is also called the American Thrush.

"Astral Tryst": This poem was originally published under the title "Astral Tryst with Several Lines from Apollinaire" in the *Mid-American Review*. Some of the quotes are twisted into the narrative using partial lines from Donald Revell's amazing translation of Guillaume Apollinaire's *Alcools*.

"Your Baby Ain't Sweet like Mine": The title is borrowed from a Carolina Chocolate Drops song who in turn borrowed it from John Lee Hooker who in turn borrowed it from . . . ? It was originally published in the *Massachusetts Review* under the title "03/04."

Shahid: "Farewell" refers to Agha Shahid Ali's poem "Farewell," and the line "my memory keeps getting in the way of our history" refers to a similar line from his poem.

American Thrush: "I Want to Do Right but Not Right Now": "I Want to Do Right but Not Right Now" is from Gillian Welch's song "Look at Miss Ohio" off her album *Soul Journey*. The quote "fingers, thumbs, / monkeys hum, monkeys beating on a drum . . ." is a paraphrase of a 1969 version of Al Perkins's children's book *Hand, Hand, Fingers, Thumb*. "I don't want to talk about the reasons I don't want to talk about the reasons I don't want to talk" is derived from the song "Ada" by the band The National. "If I speak with the words of other men" is derived from Corinthians 13:1 in the New Testament, which is translated several ways but basically goes, "If I speak in the tongues of men and of other Angels, but have not love, I am a sounding brass, a clanging cymbal."

"*Flirt*": "Without love I am a noisy going, a clanging cymbol" is again derived from Corinthians 13:1. See previous note—this line completes the quote started in the previous poem.

"Ocean Park #79": The title of this poem is taken from a favorite Richard Diebenkorn painting in which the poem takes place. It should be noted that there are no people in the painting, no buildings, or discernable forms of any kind. As you flip through a complete book of Diebenkorn paintings it is easy to see how he moves from structured, representational work and gradually erases the lines that distinguish things. The poem was originally published under the title "June #19" in *Hunger Mountain*.

"Amber & Embers": Is the name of a drink served at the Black Market Liquor Bar. The poem was originally published in *Pleiades* under the title "Water and Light."

"Main St.": "Borofksy's two-story clown" refers to Jonathan Borofsky's *Ballerina Clown* on Main St. in Santa Monica/Venice.

"Holoholo": In Hawaii, "holoholo" means to head off for a walk, a ride, or a sail strictly for pleasure. "Seeing Is Forgetting the Thing One Sees" is borrowed from the name of the Lawrence Weschler book on the light and space artist, Robert Irwin, titled, *Seeing Is Forgetting the Name of the Thing One Sees: A Life of Contemporary Artist Robert Irwin*.

"Flea": This poem was originally published in *Solo*, a good little journal that is now defunct, under the title, "Flea/House/Line from Pessoa." The line borrowed from Fernando Pessoa is no longer a part of the poem.

"For . . .": The first two lines of the poem are from Larry Levis's "For Zbigniew Herbert, Summer, 1971, Los Angeles."

ACKNOWLEDGMENTS

Grateful acknowledgment is made to the editors of the following journals in which these poems first appeared in different forms: *Art/Life*, *Barrow Street*, *Crazyhorse*, *The Harvard Review*, *The Fish Anthology*, *The Hunger Mountain Review*, *The Massachusetts Review*, *Mid-American Review*, *Open City*, *Orion*, *Pleiades*, *Rivendell*, *Solo*, and *Snake Nation Review*.

Grateful acknowledgment is also made to Billy Collins for selection as an Honorable Mention in the *Fish Anthology*.

Grateful acknowledgment is made to Donald Revell and Suzanna Tamminen for permission to use the lines from Donald Revell's translation of Guillame Apollinaire's *Alcools*.

I wish to thank the following: Squaw Valley Community of Writers for creating an amazing community in which to write as well as for a scholarship. The University of Massachusetts–Amherst, for fellowships. Of my teachers I would like to thank, specifically, Robert Hass and Yusef Komunyakaa for their generosity; Agha Shahid Ali in memorium for well, so much; and Chris Merrill for unwavering mentorship and friendship.

Special thanks to my dear friends and first readers on many of these poems: Anthony Lacavaro, Daniel Mahoney, Herman Fong, Marty Williams, Elena Karina Byrne, Ralph Angel, Chris Merrill, and Forrest Hamer (aka The Reverend)—you kept me sane. For suggestions on this project I would also like to thank, again, Elena Karina Byrne and Marty Williams.

And a thousand thank yous to Kevin Prufer. Not only have you been a great reader and editor, but you've also been a great friend

Thanks to my dad, Joseph Blaustein, for filling my life and thousands of other lives with art and kindness.

This book simply would not have happened without the unyielding support and love of my wife, Cristina Amaya. This book is for you. And, now, our beautiful children.

Thank you to Elise McHugh and the staff at the University of New Mexico Press for all your efforts in bringing this book together.